The World according to Betty

Life with a little ego

Ernestine van der Griendt

First print

by HappyMinds

(http://happyminds.nl)

ISBN: 978-94-92384-01-0

Contents

Preface

"Delighted to make your acquaintance!" "Let me introduce myself, Betty, the ego of Ernestine". "This book is about ME! "Ha-ha! I can't deny that I'm rather proud of it". "Wouldn't you be?" "Honest... no come on... honestly?" "There you go, you would be!" "Well that's nothing to be ashamed of." "Oh and don't worry, it's not just another self-help book with exercises, worksheets, action steps and theories which most people will have forgotten about at the end of the book." "No, nothing of the sort." What kind of book is it? Exceptional question!

It's an inspiration book. You can read it, have an opinion on it and extract insights if they came to you while reading this book. Things that made you think: "Oh, yes that makes sense." Or you just let it be. It's up to you, dear reader. So... That takes some pressure of your shoulders, doesn't it?

Well, a book without a purpose is a bit awkward, don't you think? So if there were to be a purpose it would be the following: "Look at me, Betty. Look at the influence I seem to have due to all the emotions I can't control and look at how I make life so much more difficult than one would choose it to be, if it were solely up to them. "But that's not my fault!" "No, I'm not to blame!" "Of course that's other people's fault. But to get that, you would have to see and recognize me. That's a happy thought! I love to be seen, seriously, I do!"

You just met Betty. It's obvious that the attitude and way of speaking slightly differs when the ego is active. While reading the book you will come to understand who Betty is, how she was born and which adventures I have had with and because of her.

"Hm, I need to get something of my chest…"

"Yes, Betty?"

"I want to apologize upfront to all the people who may feel as though they were attacked or offended. I mean, it certainly was my intention to do so – that's my job as a professional ego – but most of the time I do feel remorse after my uncontrollable urge to express my emotions. However… by that time the damage has been done and Ernestine has some work cut out for her in the damage control department, due to my actions. I apologize, meapculpa and what people tend to say in situations like these. I can't promise it will never happen again, but I will certainly try my best.

Introduction

"Why is it that I don't like you?" I asked a man on whom I secretly had a crush. I couldn't stand him because of the arrogant attitude he displayed. He looks at me and I see his surprise. He obviously didn't see that remark coming; me neither, to be honest. It just popped out. It was going to be a moment to remember. From that moment on, Betty was a fact. "Delighted to meet you! I'm Betty! Ego in full glory and in everyone's face, with the ability to fill a room with my presence and don't even think about ignoring me!"

Once we recovered from the first shock about my remark, we looked at each other and started to laugh. It sure was kind of a weird thing to say to someone you have never met in person. We started a great conversation about how we had communicated so far and what the reason was for not liking each other. Suddenly we had this crazy plan to give our egos a character; to make them visible but in a funny way. The whole subject of the ego isn't something people like to chew on.

I bet if I were to walk out into the street and ask people

if they know their ego, the majority would say "Well...
me... I don't have one", or "Well I don't think mine is that
big..."

The ego is seen as something dark and often associated
with the word egoism. In our society that is not a 'quality'
you would like to be given on your life's resume. Egois-
tic people aren't hip, and mostly not wanted. As humans
we're supposed to be nice and kind and care about others.
Loving yourself too much is 'not done'.

An hour after the 'birth' of my Betty, a group of like-mind-
ed people were sitting at a table, laughing loudly. My ego
got Betty Boop as a character. The man with whom this
whole adventure started crowned himself Peter Pan.
Across the table Pipi Longstocking was babbling cheer-
fully and Miss Piggy made some irritating noises. What
a party! An ego party, where people acknowledged their
egos and were having fun with it.

Once I told people about my Betty I got confused stares
and some even gave me advice about where to get some
useful self-help books. "You're not suffering from multiple personality disorder, are you?" was one of the reactions I got after introducing my Betty. No! I'm not. I can
assure you. I'm just becoming aware of my emotional inside world. That is what Betty stands for. All the emotions
a human may have bottled up in one small character,
standing there before you to look at. It's a helicopter view
for yourself. You can see the emotions without being part
of them. I can tell you, it's both shocking and hilarious.

It's been ten years since the day Betty was 'born' and we've
both been in training. I have come to know her well and

The World According to Betty

I manage to ignore her sometimes. That has been a long and straining road, with lots of adventures. I can laugh about them as I look back. She still bothers me sometimes... for example when I started writing this book.

The ultimate challenge. Writing a book. Of course my Betty had her opinion about that. I saw it coming. Often when I start something new, she comes and whispers arguments in my ear. Why we shouldn't do it, why it's much safer to let things be and oh... keeping things the way they are is one of her favourite subjects to talk about.

As you read this book, you will notice that I refer to Betty as 'she' and I talk about 'us' and 'we'. I like to write in this way to emphasize the presence of the ego. I know I am Betty and I'm responsible for what is being said. I wanted to point that out, just to make sure you know I'm not blaming anyone else for some of the situations I found myself in on my adventures with Betty.

As I walk through a book store, my eye catches all the books on the table. All the people who have been able to write one and then I hear my Betty's little voice, my personal inner critic: "Can you picture our book on this table between all the other books about 'awareness'?" "Is the world waiting for a book about a little ego?" "Isn't that rather arrogant of us, to think we could pull that off?" The reason Betty asks these questions is to check if I think I'm good enough, if people will actually want to buy what I wrote. She fills me up with insecurity and doubts.

Betty is a complex being, the director of my own little drama theatre. I have given her a test by writing blogs about her, so she could get used to the idea. If you want something really bad, the first thing to do is: start believing you will get it. It's not easy if the star of the book starts sabotaging the creative process by her focus on failure. Convincing Betty of the idea of 'Yes. I can!' was a challenge.

The Betty blogs are a hit. Betty is hot! People like her. She is the personification of all my emotions which everyone can relate to.

This book is a way of sharing my world (and Betty's) to inspire people. The main thing I have learned through my adventures with Betty is, that people are responsible for their thoughts and emotions. Once you discover what the ego is and does, and learn to accept that, life becomes much more pleasurable. Well, I can't think of anyone who wouldn't like to have a life which is fulfilling and enjoyable.

Like all great writers, I would like to thank all the people I have come across and with whom I have argued or debated. Thank you for the experience. Thank you letting me get to know Betty.

Chapter 1 What does yours look like?

"A book… about your ego, you've got to be kidding", says a friend. I laughed: "Sure, about my Betty". "Did you pick your character yet?" "Well, I don't know about that", he mumbles. "How do you pick one?" "Well, you know what your face looks like if you have an emotion, do you?' I explain. "For example, if you're offended, disappointed or just plain pissed off". My friend giggles, while I continue: "What character from a cartoon can you find that resembles what you look like at these moments?"

It seemed to be a tough question and I could imagine his struggle. Picking a character for the ego means that you have to acknowledge the fact that you actually have one. That is a brave thing to do. Realizing that this ego stands for all your emotions and admitting that you have an ego is like standing naked in front of mankind. We'd rather be seen as the amicable neighbour, the loving mother, the ideal daughter in law, etc.

"But what does the ego stand for?" my friend asks while

he still struggled with his search for a character.

Ego is Latin for "I". You might think that you are your ego, but that isn't quite true. The ego is just a part of you. I always see it as the little voice inside my head. The stream of thoughts you have during a situation you happen to come across. It's the way you think about yourself and about others. You could say it's your inner critic, your own bodyguard. These are all things the ego is good at. The ego isn't something you would want to get rid of. It is a very functional part of us.

Every day we have experiences. We look at the world around us, we interpret what we experience and we have an opinion on it. A good example might be getting feedback at work. Someone is saying something about you and your qualities. That's not a big problem until something negative is being said about you. "Points of improvement". The ego starts working on that. Words are being filtered, looked at, and translated. A feeling about the words starts to develop. Nobody likes hearing less positive things about themselves. The reaction that arises within us after such a moment, is the creation of the ego.

The ego is responsible for the way you judge yourself. If you aren't very positive about yourself, or even insecure and people suggest 'points of improvement' to you, you'll most likely experience a strong emotion about it. This may vary from anger, sadness, disappointment, self-judgement or even the urge to strike back at the messenger.

You might say that we are responsible for our own behaviour or reactions to feedback. Over the last years I've been experimenting with this. My ego had a resistance to this way of thinking. "Yes... but that man said some really awful things about us and he spoke those words", I hear Betty say. "So we've got to accept that we are responsible for what he is saying?"

At that point I didn't get that the words someone speaks can only hurt me if I let them hurt me. That only happens if I decide to see other people's opinion as THE truth. If I'm convinced of my own qualities and feel good about myself, the words won't hurt me that easily.

On the day I started to realize that my ego had a bit too much influence on my behaviour, my adventure with Betty started. A long exploring trip to watch myself and try to grow as a person, began. I had read so many self-help books, that I had become tired of reading them. All the advises and action plans I couldn't stick to made me have a talk with my little ego.

It became a way of looking at myself and my struggles from a distance and discovering why I did the things I did. The biggest answer to where my behaviour came from was simply: the right of existence.

"Why did you choose Betty Boop?" my friend wants to know. "You don't have black hair and, no offence intended, but your figure isn't quite the hourglass shape that Betty has..." I laughed and said: "Look... you just put your finger on the right spot". "I'm not my ego, so she may look different from me". "Betty was picked because of the diva look. That's how I feel when I'm emotional. It's like being a little sobbing lady who doesn't get her way. A lady who thinks she has a right to other people's attention, their complete attention and she means right now! The appearance of Betty has nothing to do with me as a person.

"Do you like… to talk to this Betty of yours?" My friend doesn't seem to get enough of the Betty questions. "Well, I don't talk to her out loud". Betty is a way to monitor my emotions. My friends have become used to her and find her an easy way to point out that I'm in an emotional state again. It's easier than asking if it's that time of the month again.

The whole idea of the character is making life easier for me and enabling me to reflect on my reactions towards others to learn from it. The ego is the part of us that wants to prevent things. It wants to make sure that we aren't in any danger, that big changes are being avoided or that we get the recognition we deserve, according to the ego. You'd almost think that it's a bit of a childish part of us humans. Jealousy, greed, revenge, it's all in there; in our egos.

"But why would you even consider writing a book about it: You show things, personal things which we usually keep to ourselves: Things that people may use against you at a certain point". He grinned. "Are you aiming for social loneliness, or what?" My friend is worried about the effect that sharing my story will have on the world.

"Now look", I say, "People will always have an opinion about what I say or do". "How they'll read this book, I don't know. My Betty has an opinion about the whole book thing, of course. You should hear her… She has asked me the same questions you just did. If I would listen to my ego all the time, I would never be able to do spontaneous things. I may as well put my creativity in boxes and store them in the garage. I would have to adjust my behaviour to a standard that is acceptable to society. That won't make me happy."

"Yes, I do show a lot about my personal life. The shadow sides of a human being, the ugly side, the person one would be when no one is looking. Luckily I know that everyone has this little person inside them. Yes they do, everyone does! One may deny it, but I know better. I think being vulnerable is a way of being powerful. Besides, wanting to please the whole human race is a goal that cannot be achieved, so I won't even go there."

"What is your goal when it comes to the book?" my friend wants to know. "Did you pick your character yet?" I ask teasingly. "No…" "Quite the challenge eh…"

I want to inspire the world. It is inspiring to me to share things that were helpful for me and throwing them on the table for other people to look at. They may do with it as they please. I'm not the great wise one, I've no PHD in Ego logics, but I'm just my own guinea pig in the search of how the ego works.

There are numerous self-help books in the world, so I thought I wanted to do something different for a change. An Inspiration Book, as you wish; if you want to help yourself, of course, because that's up to you. I believe you can't help people by telling them what to do. If someone doesn't see the point of changing, they may try, but success isn't guaranteed.

What people may get from my book…? Maybe they will recognize things by reading my adventures and maybe they will be inspired to get their own Betty and start talking to her. It may make life a bit easier.

I know my Betty has been a great tool to monitor myself. I'm not always able to master my ego, sometimes it takes a short break and a deep breath. As to where I used to go into battle fully armed, nowadays I let things be for a short while and take time to think. That way the emotion will get smaller and I can look at things from a different perspective.

"What do others who are close to you think of your Betty?" my friend asks. "Well usually they have fun with Betty". It gives them a tool to confront me with my emotions without getting into a fight. Saying something like: "Betty is awake, I assume?" will do the trick.

"Isn't this Betty character a smart way of avoiding taking responsibility for your own actions?" "You can always say… ah, well Betty did it, but she is a part of you, as you explained to me…" "You are absolutely right, Betty is a part of me. I'm well aware of her, but I know it is me driving the car, not her. I'm responsible for my actions at all times".

"How do you start a book?" "If I were to try I wouldn't know where to start and how to put things in to chapters." "I've been wanting to write a book for some time now and honestly, I had no clue as to how to go about it." "Having a Betty looking over your shoulder is an extra challenge, I can tell you. The ego is the master in doubting your own abilities. I had some practice with writing blogs about Betty and that was fun, but a complete book… wow, that's a whole different story."

I have written lots of little stories about Betty and there always was a theme. Once I started thinking about what to put in the book I made a list of things I've been working on with my Betty. I wanted to make a chapter of each of those subjects and share the adventure I experienced.

"How does Betty fit in a relationship? I mean, how do you explain talking to your ego, which is a character, to your date?" "I love your question!" I answer smiling. "Let me tell you, my boyfriend has his own character." "You didn't think I'd settle for a guy who doesn't acknowledge his ego?" I think it has made the relationship more open and honest, using the characters, but I won't spoil the fun! You can read about it in the book…"

Chapter 2 Top 10

So, there I was, aware of the little diva in my head. What to do with your own little character? Great question!

My life got more complex than it was before my Betty was born. Not being aware of the ego was so much easier, because suddenly a challenging little character is there and you get to see exactly what you have been up to. That's not always fun to watch, even rather painful at times.

Betty showed a mix of what an ego can do. It judges, is not pleased with things or situations, seeks attention, wants to be in control and says things you afterwards often wished you hadn't said. Betty is a pile of feelings and convictions. I made a top 10 of all she can be.

BETTY'S TOP 10

IMPATIENT
DEMANDING
ANGER
FEAR
NEED TO BE SAFE
SELF PITTY
JUDGEMENTAL
NEED FOT ATTENTION
NO COMPASSSION
NEED TO BE RIGHT

You could say "Go away Betty!" "Be gone", if all the ego does is causing trouble. You'd rather be the most loving, caring, funny and enjoyable person you can be? Yes… But Betty isn't just my ugly side. There are advantages.

Take the writing of this book for example. Betty had her opinion on that. She threw large amounts of insecurity at me. "It's scary, writing a book." "We reveal a lot about ourselves." Funny enough, I had a conversation with a great coach and he made me look at my passion. After that it was Betty who put on her boxing gloves and shouted: "Let's get this show on the road, darling!" "Let's show the world what we are capable of." She got triggered by a flow of confidence and wanted to make this happen.

The ego isn't all bad. It can also stimulate you when you get challenged: the 'I'm going to make this work-effect'. It's combining forces for good or bad purposes. It works both ways.

So a positive top 10 of Betty can be put together as well.

BETTY'S TOP 10

INDEPENDANT

SELF CONFIDENCE

COURAGE

PRIDE

FEELS SECURE

SELF APPRECIATION

TAKES HER TIME

PERSERVERANCE

KNOWS WHAT
SHE WANTS

TAKES GOOD
CARE OF
HERSELF

Besides all the 'dark' sides of the ego, an opposite site can be found, which you may prove to be useful.

After I met Betty it seemed like I had entered a boot camp with one goal: turning around my thoughts. The negative ones. That wasn't easy. The ideas and convictions I had built up so carefully over the past forty years were still very active.

It helped to write blogs about it for my friends; telling them about what I saw through Betty's eyes, including the less attractive sides. It was like a camera crew from a real life soap following me around. At the end of the day I could watch the show to see what I had been up to. Luckily I had the ability to laugh about it after reading my own story. Humour is a very good way to see things in another perspective.

An extra effect of getting to know your ego is that you start recognizing the egos of others. Betty soon came across many little 'friends'. Other people's egos were like a baby boom after the war. There were many times where Betty bumped in to one of them. Other people didn't like her saying "You have an ego too you know? Yes, you do!"

Not everyone wanted to pick a character to start a course in self-reflection. The ironic part was, that I myself had a strong dislike for people who wanted to change the world and thought they had the right to tell others how to change things about themselves.

One day a friend asked me: "Are you happy?" After thinking about it I replied: "Yes, I am." "That's impossible!" "Look at your life!" the friend said. He produced a complete list of all the things that were wrong with my life and that it was absolutely impossible for me to be a happy person, considering the circumstances.

Betty had moved to the edge of her little couch to get a better view from the panorama window she has in my head. It seemed there was an 'enemy' approaching us. Analysing people is Betty's job and she's not particularly fond of being subjected to it herself. I looked at the friend and said "That's true, however, happiness is always a moment in time and lucky for me there is always at least one moment of happiness to be found in my day".

The conversation continued and my friend got more hostile by the minute (and Betty was doing karate moves on top of the bench). "So you want me to believe that it's ME who's responsible for my feelings?" In her role as 'miss know it all' Betty had stated that people are only able to feel hurt if they allow others to do so. That statement pushed my friend over the edge.

Oh dear, Betty had started a mini war by selling her life lessons to others and not being very compassionate. She put her foot in her mouth again. The next thing I knew, the subject had changed to having expectations. "Expectations can only lead to disappointment" I heard myself say. That was the last straw. My friend went wild. "There are certain rules and standards in life, you know! It's common behaviour to obey those rules and thus normal for me to have those expectations" he said with a face turning red with outrage. You mean to say that I'm not normal for wanting you to act like everyone else?" During his rage I wished I hadn't let Betty play the all-knowing creature she so loved to play. I tried to explain that having expectations isn't the issue, the disappointment afterwards is.

If you want people to act in a certain way, that's fine, but if they don't satisfy your expectations that's your problem. You can't make people behave the way you would like them to do. You can be disappointed, but how you react from there on is your choice.

My friend was upset. How on earth could I pretend such rubbish? Betty was getting ready to throw any sharp object she could get her hands on at the friend. I decided it was time to stop the battle. "Maybe you're right", I started. "Oh no, now we're playing let's say he's right and be done with it? Oh no, that's too easy! That's like starting a fire and running away without taking responsibility for the fire!" Now who's the coward here? I had to use every nerve in me to restrain Betty. I was being triggered at the highest level. "You know, I don't like the way this conversation is going and I understand you're upset with me, but I'm stopping this right now!" With the last bit of self-control in my body I turned around and walked away. Sometimes it's better to leave the battle before it gets out of hand.

It took me some time before I could control Betty in her urge to sell her life lessons to others. It wasn't doing our social status in life much good.

Chapter 3 The Pity Party

In my 'poor me phase' everyone seemed to have more money, a nicer house and a successful relationship. My focus (and Betty's) was mainly on what we didn't have. If you pay attention to things, they become bigger. So what happened… I got less of what I so desperately wanted.

Before I knew Betty well, she was the leading lady in my every day theatre. She was convinced that the world was cold and mean and that she was always the victim.

Betty felt very sorry for herself, because things didn't work out on the dating circuit. The problem with that attitude is that it doesn't stop. It is a self-fulfilling prophecy. The poor-me-person Betty had become, put bars around our love life. It didn't make us attractive or desirable. We had no clue that we had done that all by ourselves. No, blaming men was a far better excuse. Men were no good anyway, so there you have it! (That was Betty…)

The solution to this problem was right in front of me: changing my way of thinking about the situation, but Betty wasn't ready to cooperate. The Americans have a great saying for it. "Celebrating your pity party". It's a lonesome party, for one person. You!

Tax bills seemed to find my mail box in a flowing stream. Year after year I had to pay extra taxes and the company I owned started to die slowly. Part of the cause was my way of thinking, but Betty didn't think so.

Many times Betty sat on her queen-size window seat in front of the panorama window in my head. Sighing. Looking at all the other people who seemed to get everything they desired.

If only I had known sooner that Betty was writing a fairy tale causing my lack of success… "Unhappily ever after." She could recite chapters with drama for hours. "What have you done with your life? There you are… forty years old with a company on life support, no chance of a steady income. A roof above your head, but for how long?" Panic was the dominating emotion within Betty. "What if we become homeless?" she whispered anxiously.

It was at moments like these, I sat at my table and took a deep breath and another one… and another one. The funny thing was, if I kept doing that, Betty seemed to calm down. Out of the blue, an idea came up and a little miracle seemed to happen. A little stream of money entered our life and we kept a roof over our heads.

Of course Betty had her opinion on that. "It's not a structural solution!" "How are we going to get by after this miracle?" At moments like these I thought: "Oh shut up, will you!"

A broad variety of self-help books was catching dust on

my bookshelf. One of the books that was very helpful to me was the one on turning around thoughts. Not an easy task, with Betty always 'helping 'me with what to think or what not to think. One of the exercises was The Mirror Work.

Step one: Go stand in front of the mirror and look at yourself. Step two: Say "I like myself" to yourself. That was it! Betty had enough and started giving me a peace of her mind: "Yeah, sure… telling yourself you are nice." "Are you kidding me?" "That's daft." "No way we are going to do this." "It's fine that we want attention, but we'll get that from other people with an opinion that counts for something." "No way we are going to starting liking ourselves in front of a mirror." "Get real!"

That wasn't going to work, with a resisting Betty. My creative way of thinking was still working, even with Betty around. I started using the world as my mirror.

The stories I wrote for my friends were a good start. Telling them about who I was. I could be vulnerable in a safe environment. The reactions were great and people could relate to my Betty.

I had to solve the 'liking yourself-task' in a different way. I started to tell others "Well, I woke up this morning and guess what, I was so adorable." People started laughing and said: "Really, how wonderful." It was cheating, I know. I used the world to convince myself, but hey I had Betty to fool…

After a while, I started to believe that I actually was a great person, sometimes (I hadn't won the battle with Betty yet). It seemed like the 'poor me attitude' had everything to do with how I felt about myself. Self-appreciation, self-worth, and all elements I seemed to have a lack of.

I once read that it takes twenty-one days before something becomes a habit. It took me more than twenty-one days to start liking me.

In the meantime the money problem kind of solved itself, my living situation was secured. That left one issue for Betty to chew on… the nice relationship.

Growing up with castle novels in my teenage hands, my view on relationships was slightly coloured. Of course I saw the deeply romanticized way a woman met a man on page one. Of course I noticed that it took her about a hundred pages to get involved with him, only to lose track of him and catch up on the last page to express her eternal love. But hey, it felt good to read those stories.

Reality was far less romantic and it took me an entire encyclopaedia to find my prince charming. Till death do us part. We never got that far, we got divorced after twelve years. At thirty-eight I was going through life with a 'single' status.

One day I was sitting looking at my computer when an advertisement for a dating site caught my eye. My curiosity made my finger click on the button. Welcome to the relationship planet… for free free free. Well, if it's for free, why not look around?

I soon found out that nothing was for free, free, free there. You had to fill out all sorts of forms before being allowed to go and snoop. I was part of the naive race.

The World According to Betty

I sat watching with my eyes filled with astonishment. It looked like an online shopping guide. Something got over me. Something I usually don't approve of...

Betty looked from her panorama window with an ugly face shouting: "Next, next, next!" "Oh not that one, not that one oh... definitely not that one!" I was shocked by my own behaviour.

I turned the pages on the virtual shopping guide and looked at how all these men presented themselves. Some with a picture, some without one. Some with a lot of words in their introduction, some without hardly any.

I'd only been on this planet a few minutes when a little screen popped up. A picture and a message that some man wanted to say something to me. Huh? I hadn't quite figured out the do's and don'ts so I didn't know what to do. I clicked on the screen to be polite.

"IEEE!" Betty yelled. I wasn't very happy about the face that was staring at me from the picture. Instantly I thought that this was such a rude way to react. Out of stress I clicked on the DELETE button and the man had been erased. That planet was something else... I kept feeling amazed about all the possibilities. There were so many options. "How would you like your date, madam...?" "Tall, short, dark, blue eyes, and what zodiac sign..." Unbelievable.

I filled in some options and –plonk 362– male inhabitants of the planet came to the surface. Well, I'd better make some coffee, I thought. This is going to take some time. I was impressed with all the things these men had written down about themselves. Naivety was something I left behind me from that moment on.

The men weren't charming and one of the main goals seemed to be 'fast and easy' instead of 'long and happily ever after'. A large percentage of the men already had a female companion sitting on their couch. They were trying to find a way to add parts that seemed to be lacking in their existing relationships. They also were very picky in their preferences concerning looks, as was I (I admit it).

The relation planet was too much for me and Betty. We left in a hurry, leaving the 362 men in their own world.

A feeling of longing stayed. Being alone was hard sometimes and that made me try again. The encyclopaedia of my love stories was growing.

In the encounters with men Betty and I often met other egos. That would lead to remarkable situations. I remember meeting a man who also had a character for his ego and he called him Henri.

Betty was thrilled to meet Henri. But the awareness of the ego wasn't a guarantee for a successful relationship. Not long after the first date Betty found herself in a battle with Henri.

The fridge (a totally innocent piece of machinery) was the cause of a massive quarrel. "You shouldn't keep your bananas in the fridge" said Henri when he had opened the door of the fridge. Not really something to get pissed off about, but Betty saw the expression on his face and heard a tone in his voice. She walked up to the fridge, looked inside and felt a rogue flow inside her. She took a deep breath and said: "Those are MY bananas. In MY fridge."

Henri wasn't that easily impressed and continued his story. "Yes, well, but I worked at a grocery store and I know for sure it's bad for the bananas." Betty took another deep breath, took the bananas out of the fridge, threw them on a plate and left them in the kitchen. As she walked away from this scene she heard Henri say "You're out of cola!"

Henri sat down on the sofa and started watching television. As Betty passed him he asked "Is there something bothering you?" "No, nothing at all". One second later she says: "Yes, actually there is something! I want to be able to put my bananas in my fridge and yes I know I'm out of cola!"

The rest of the evening Henri sat quietly on the sofa. Betty was behind the computer and thought: 'Is this what it's like when you've just met a man? Is this a flashback? This is supposed to be fun? Why is the television turned on anyway? Why is he sitting on the sofa like he's lived here for years? Why is he poking his nose in where I keep my bananas? Why is he here at all?' Betty had reached the limit.

Because of my ego I learned that I liked to be free. The banana incident made me realize I didn't want someone to share my space. I felt limited in my way of living. Boy, that was a revelation after having the idea of not being able to be alone.

Looking back on it, the situation was extremely funny. Of course Betty was over reacting on the banana story. She started to defend our way of living and was flabbergasted by the way Henri made himself at home after knowing us for such a short time.

Henri didn't make it as a potential prince charming. Betty was too much for him. Once I wanted to create some space between the two egos, Henri went crazy. I apologized for my behaviour, but Henri wasn't done yet. He kept on whining and wanted to point out how badly he was treated. That was it! Betty's little finger reached for the Block this contact-button. Sorry Henri, kindergarten is over and Betty is done with you!

In the search for love a friend recommended to make a list. A list with all the things we would like to see in a man. Well, guess who started looking for a pen and paper in a hurry... right, Betty! She spent days filling the list. Not a single detail was to be left out. It felt like a package of parts to build the perfect model.

The ego seems to make choices based on old experiences. The list was filled with 'not that type again'. A man with a strong ego, been there, done that! A man with a soft and dreamy character, not our cup of tea. Betty ate him for breakfast. The awareness fanatic who wanted to reform us, not very pleasant. Betty still jumps into a karate pose by the mentioning of his name. For me, these experiences were valuable lessons. If you have 'bad' experiences, at least you know what you don't want any more. It will bring you closer to what you do want.

Betty had a protecting role in our search for Mr. Right. She set boundaries, was my bodyguard, my detective for men with less noble intentions. The little diva who explained to married men that she was adorable for the entire 365 days a year and not just at times where his calendar had some blanks or when his wife had gone to Zumba class.

It was a remarkable journey, letting go of the pity party. All the difficult moments did contribute to me realizing that I have a say in what happens in my life and Betty needed to be quiet.

Chapter 4 Fear-filled Betty

If I ask myself today if I'm easily scared, the answer is no. I'm a tough cookie. If there is a difficult situation, I tend to face it. Betty is a strong believer in getting things over with.

Being scared, in my opinion, has to do with making assumptions on what might happen. So once again thoughts are a huge influence on how you feel. For example starting your own business is often a struggle due to fear. The ego comes up with all sorts of thoughts that make you doubt your plans. 'Can we pay the rent if we become an entrepreneur? Will we survive owning a business? Will people like what we're offering?'

This doubt is based on insecurity. Fear and insecurity go hand in hand in this negative thinking spiral. Where do these ideas come from anyway? Why can't we just think that we are an awesome person?

According to psychologists we'll find the answers to that in our childhood, because somewhere during our upbringing we pick up beliefs about not being good enough.

I'm sure our parents got their beliefs the same way, so it's a system that is passed on from generation to generation.

If a mother has a fear for spiders and acts upon that on a regular basis, her children will believe that being afraid of spiders is the appropriate way to think. I think doing some research on the beliefs of your parents might shed some light on your beliefs and fears. A trip down memory lane may pay off.

My mother had an issue with driving a car. I got my driver's licence at eighteen. It was a present for my graduation. So, there I was; eighteen years old, with the ability to drive without a car. I lived in a big city, where the bus or a bike were the common way of transportation. Anyway, thirteen years later, living in a small village, with a car parked outside, I decided to take a refreshers course. Five lessons, to get started again.

I was a stay at home mother with a one year old child, so being able to drive would give me more freedom to go see people. After the lessons I was driving again, but I noticed that other drivers bothered me. I had met the 'tailgaters'. They freaked me out. Betty was sitting next to me in the car and made remarks. Non-stop. "Move over to the other lane!" "They are pushing us." "Let's take the alternative road next time, it's a jungle out here!"

That would have been the only problem, if it hadn't been for that one single incident. I was waiting for a traffic light on a road that was a bit steep. As I pulled up I had no idea that the road was so steep and before I knew it, my car was sliding down slowly towards the car behind me. I was freaking out. The car behind me was filled with construction builders who were laughing at me for being so silly.

Betty made sure that I put this experience in the archive under the letter D for Dangerous. My behaviour was then adjusted to avoiding all roads where we could possibly get in to the same situation. No more steep roads for us.

That was a bit tricky, because the world isn't entirely flat. You do occasionally bump in to slopes and often when you expect it the least. After a visit to the hospital I found myself facing a road that went downhill and up again. At that point there was a traffic jam, so I had to stop. Looking in the rear-view mirror I saw a big truck coming up. Oh my goodness, what was I to do? I would surely bump in to that truck. I never prayed, but there and then I became a firm believer. I called upon all the angels and gods in the sky! Asking for help to get me out of that situation. I sat there frozen. If I were to take my foot of the brake, I would roll down. I hadn't practiced the use of the hand brake during my lessons. I decided to let the cars in front of me pull up and I made sure there was a big distance between me and them. Then I took my foot of the brake and pressed the gas pedal like crazy. I wanted to move! Forward, not backwards! It worked! But I was sweating and shaking.

The fear of highways and steep roads had become a serious issue. Until the day I wanted to go to a training on changing thinking patterns so very badly. I had to drive to the south of my country for that. I had tried everything to avoid driving there myself, but it looked like all the people I asked had been in an intervention meeting on my behalf. None of the people I asked were going to drive me. Betty was having a fit. It was mean and she was sure people were conspiring against us.

"Well, OK, we'll drive ourselves then!" she said. Preparing for the polar trip of which I was sure we were going to make , I thought of everything. Water, a blanket, food, my little card for the emergency road service, just in case. There I went, on to the highway. The trip went smooth up to the point when my GPS Navigation stopped talking to me. 'What?? Not now! Please, woman in the little box, speak! I'm never going to arrive if you give me the silent treatment!'

Somewhere in the panic of that moment Betty saw a sign with a city name. I knew that city was located in the direction where I was heading. I decide to take that exit. The heroic thought of Betty immediately changed into the critical flow of thinking. What if we get lost? I ignored her for a while. About ten minutes before I would have had a serious problem with where to go next I heard "Take the next exit." The woman had returned from the ignoring mode." Hallelujah, I was saved.

It was a good thing she came back, given the fact that I'm known for my talent of choosing the wrong direction. The GPS Navigation was my life saving system, at least as long as she was on speaking terms with me...

Once I got to the Bed and Breakfast I was shaking. I just crossed four states. Four states! That was amazing! I called my coach and left him a message. Like Rocky Balboa standing on top of the stairs I felt a victory in me. I made it!

The World According to Betty

(Yes. Of course I had booked a Bed and Breakfast. Imagine having to get through traffic in the morning with all the jams. I don't think Betty and I would have lived to tell that story...)

The next day I entered the conference room where the training took place. Funny how emotions can be bottled up for a while. During the introduction round I felt nervous. It was my turn to introduce myself and before I knew it I was having an emotional breakdown.

Small detail I think is worth mentioning, I was at an NLP training (Neuro Linguistic Programming) where you learn to bend old beliefs into new beliefs. The trainer walked up to me and took me to the middle of the room. I sat on a chair and he started talking to me, while I was having trouble breathing due to all the stress from the adventure I had experienced the day before. He wiggled my arms while talking to me. Suddenly he said: "Let's go outside!"

I saw a very expensive looking car parked and the trainer opened the door. "Take a seat", he said while holding the door at the driver's seat. I mumbled something about "expensive car" and not knowing why I had to get in.

The trainer got in at the passenger seat and his assistant sat in the back. I wondered why he had come with us.. Just in case, they told me. "Start the car", I heard. "Is this a diesel?" I asked terrified. "Yes, wonderful car, isn't it?" Betty went crazy. No way, we were going to drive in a diesel car. No way, not ever! We only drive gas. And another thing, what if we drive this wonderful and very expensive car into a ditch? And why is this man thinking we'll be able to get it driving anyway? "Go on, start the car", the trainer said.

The car slowly started to move. It was like the car was having a hiccup. The two men in the car were being shaken due to my inexperience at driving a diesel. To make things even scarier, a snowstorm had just decided to join us. I was sitting in the car, almost with my nose glued to the window trying to stay on the road. "How was your experience with giving birth to your child?" the trainer asked out of the blue. "My delivery???" "Well, eh…" I started to tell the story. After fifteen minutes the trainer said "You do realize, you are driving a diesel, in a snowstorm?" I looked at him and then it hit me. Holy cow! I was driving a diesel… in a snowstorm!

After this victory I sat next to a man. He introduced himself as the owner of a skidpan. He said: "Girl, you come and see me at my school." "I'll help you get rid of your fear of steep roads." That was a promise I really liked.

After reading my story of driving in the snow, you'll agree with me that this trainer was a bit weird, wouldn't you? I didn't know it could get even weirder. I discovered that in the evening. He stopped by to give me a paper to sign. A waiver. I was asked to sign so he couldn't be held responsible for anything that might happen during that evening. Betty didn't like it at all. Not knowing what was coming and having to sign a waiver for it?

As I entered the room, mumbo jumbo music was played. The lights were turned down and my eyes saw the big steel bars on the floor. What on earth were they going to do with those bars? Betty was having a fit. She was just about to go tell the trainer she wasn't going to join this activity as the doors closed. No way back.

I was asked to sit down and think of a situation where I felt extremely powerful. The birth of my child came to mind again. That was an experience that I would not forget for as long as I lived. The point was, to focus on the feeling you had at the point and store it somewhere inside so you could access it again later on. It was to be an anchor for power.

The trainer then explained what the bars where for. Two people would be standing with the bar between them, lifting the bar and putting it on their throats. After making contact with the power anchor inside, they had to walk towards each other and the bar would bend.

'Yeah, sure', Betty thought. 'Over my dead body! I decided to let others go first, to see if they would survive this challenge. To my surprise…they did. Well, if they did, I could give it a try. My heart was pounding heavily. With sweaty hands I stood there. Ready to do this. The steel bar felt cold on my throat made me want to run away, but I just stood there, frozen. Thousands of thoughts went through my mind. I looked at the person at the end of the bar and he nodded. Oh my goodness, we were going to do this! I thought of my anchor and started walking. And the bar… bent! Yes! I was doing it!

After that I was filled with power, joy and courage. I did it! Me, Miss scared of everything! I did it.

After this weekend I drove home in my car, with not a care in the world.

I did go and see the man from the skid pan. It was a day full of challenges. A steep road on the training field. He made me drive all the way up. Once I got there I said "I can't do this." Betty was freaking out. "Into the lifeboats!", she screamed. "We are on a steep hill!" The trainer calmly said: "Well, there's no way back, dearie, you will have to do something." I said my prayers. I didn't want to let go of the emergency brake. I saw myself going downwards with the car. Somewhere I found my anchor again. I let go of the brake and the car moved, forwards. After one hour, I was going up and down the hill, like it was the most common thing to do for me.

Overcoming beliefs that Betty had stored inside me. Lovely! What a feeling of freedom. I never felt scared of steep roads again. I was cured.

Of course Betty has lots and lots of other beliefs in her little archive. To her fear is real. Fear is thinking something is true, without having proof of it.

Fear is usually the lack of proof. Or reacting from an old experience. A humiliating experience, a failure in doing something, it influences you afterwards.

If you have the guts to test these beliefs, to look the bear in the eye (the one you put on the road yourself), you'll notice that it's mostly an illusion, the fear experience.

The thoughts you have on things you are scared about can be reversed. Driving in a diesel through a snowstorm was the ultimate test for me. The trainer distracted me by getting me to talk about a something so off topic. He tricked Betty by being unpredictable. Instead of freaking out, I told my story and proved that I could drive a diesel in a snowstorm. The focus was taken off the old belief and a new one was made.

Chapter 5 Thoughts to chew on

Betty sticks out her tongue. Bleh. "All those nice advises about emotional eating and loving yourself. Get out of here. I already love myself!"

If anyone knows the yoyo-effect when it comes to losing weight, it's me. I've had this love-hate relationship with diets. Somewhere around 2006 I was done. Done with being overweight. I'd made a deal with myself. A deadline and the number of pounds I was going to lose. That was it.

To get support from the people around me, I told everyone about my plan. The reactions weren't uplifting.

"Are you being realistic, if you want to lose twenty-two pounds in three months' time?" "Besides, why lose weight?" "You are good enough as you are now." Betty was sick and tired of it.

The lack of confidence made Betty angry. Why can't they believe in me? Why do they doubt already? I haven't even started.

With my own confidence to build on I began my project. I went to Weight Watchers meetings. They weighed me and I went home, shocked of the extra pounds that weren't there on the scale at home. Sticking to the Weight Watchers plan wasn't enough, I had to start an exercising program as well.

So I made a schedule which calculated the time I would spend on my cross-trainer. The first day was a bit like getting sober after a party. But I managed to stay on the cross-trainer for ten minutes, instead of the five I had planned.

I had been an angel all week. The first time I got weighed again I had only lost one pound. Two ladies who started at the same time as I did, lost ten pounds in a week. Betty was spitting on the floor. "Not fair!"

The deal I made with myself was still in my head and I decided to get over my disappointment and to go on. The next week I lost two pounds. "Now we're talking", I thought. Working out on the cross-trainer was getting easier too.

The people around me were harder to deal with then the diet itself. "Ah come on, woman, just one cookie won't hurt!" That's what people said as I attended a birthday at my neighbours.

Betty whispered from her own room "Which part of NO THANKS isn't getting through to you? Are you here to test us? Is it abnormal that I want to reach my goal and I don't put my teeth in your cake?"

That's why I came up with something Betty thought was

PRETTY brilliant… I went to birthdays with a little plastic bag. In that bag I had four cookies (one point on the daily list from the diet). For me four cookies were like psychological binge eating. Once the host asked me if I wanted cake, I would get my little bag out and say "No thanks, I brought my own." Eventually they gave up on asking me.

Two weeks before the deadline I reached my goal, the twenty-two pounds weight loss. Betty was thrilled. We made them eat dirt! We made it. So, now for round two. Another twenty-two pounds and a deadline. The reactions from the people around were still not supportive.

"Well, now you'll have to keep it this way." "The first pounds are the easiest to loose, then you get stuck. I don't know what it is with people. Why can't they be happy for others? Anyway, a year later the goal was reached.

One day I was walking home from the soccer field where my daughter had just played a game. The following conversation with an acquaintance took place:

"What did you do? I had to look twice to see if it was really you." For me these conversations were like talking on automatic pilot.

The answers:
YES
Weight Watchers
No, no trouble at all
No, I will keep going till it's finished

The questions:
Boy, did you lose a lot of weight?

Wow, did you do a specific diet?
Must have been hard?
You're done now?

The hard part of changing was, the people around responded to how I looked and not to me as a person. Betty couldn't handle that. "So, now I'm acceptable according to society?" The weight loss changed me from the inside as well. The ever so sweet, caring, always polite woman, had gone with all the pounds.

Sadly, the pounds returned. The years of emotional roller coasting and finding myself again gave me some extra curves. I know I did that but Betty is a partner in crime.

It starts with one cookie with my coffee. Hey, having coffee by yourself isn't always fun. So settled with the cookie to join me, a thought passes. "Hmm that tasted good." Betty starts talking. "Well, just one extra won't hurt." Remember how pissed off she was when my neighbours said it?

I go to the kitchen and I take two, because I know Betty! She will start again. Later on the package is half empty. Oh dear, that's not good for our weight. Guess who starts complaining… Right, Betty! The guilt trip she starts is killing. First she helps me to eat them and later she punishes for doing it just that…

I lost almost a hundred pounds and I have gained fifty back. I can recall my mother saying: "Now the hard part is keeping it this way." Mothers are almost always right, sadly. At that time I had some trouble listening, but I'm a good sport. She was right.

The World According to Betty

It's like a daily mind game with Betty: promising ourselves to work out. I look at the cross-trainer in my bedroom and I decide to have some coffee first. No hurry, we have all day.

Before I know it, it's 12 pm and I haven't found my way to the cross-trainer. After dinner I sigh and realize that I did actually promise to do it. Once my head hits the pillow, I promise myself to do it tomorrow.

Some time ago I put my bike in the hallway, another mind game with Betty. Now I see my bike on a regular basis, I go out to get my groceries by bike and sometimes I go into the city. Before that it was parked in the basement and I had to push it up a small hill to use it, and you all know what I was like with hills... Too much trouble; especially if the car is out front, ready to use.

Every time I look in the mirror I think back. I see myself at the point that I reached the hundred pounds weight loss. My new me! My victory! I remember how happy I felt going in to the city and walk in to any store to buy clothes. No more size plus shopping. I know I have to start working out to get those days back.

Eating is an issue and I know I'm not the only one in the world who struggles with it. Emotional eating is a theme in a lot of self-help books and this has a reason, but you can do something about this way of coping with emotions. It all starts (yes I know I'm not the first to tell you this) by loving yourself. Betty is a little rebel though, you see that by now. So, guess what she does when she hears this? Yes, she puts her tongue out towards me. Prrrrt.

Shopping is an adventure with a tag-a-long like Betty. I try to buy healthy food, but once I get in to the lane where the chocolate is to be found, an inner battle occurs. Once we are in the supermarket, the adventure starts. I want to buy healthy food and I accomplish that to some level, but the chocolate department is a must-see. I avoid shopping for groceries close to dinner time, because I know that the amount of goodies will be BIG once I reach the register.

Losing weight is not hard. If you just don't call it losing weight. Keeping fit is a different way of putting it. I know, it's all between my ears, the place where Betty lives. If she sees it as just keeping fit and eating three meals a day and the occasional snack, it might work. If I make things complicated by looking at action plans from Weight Watchers, she will put her foot down. "Hm, here we go again." "No more sweets, no delicious cookies." But so far I can deal with her. It gets worse if something bad happens and emotions are involved. That's when she's painfully present in my head, wanting my full attention. I'd better hurry to the supermarket to buy some chocolate cookies, because Betty needs comfort food.

Of course I'm the one going to the shop, the one making the decision. It's just hard to ignore the negative emotions Betty comes up with. Sometimes music will do the trick, or calling a friend. Recently I succeeded in turning the thoughts around by using my cross trainer.

It takes some effort to let go of the motion once something bad happens. Focusing on something else gives you other things to think about, so you will be distracted.

The World According to Betty

Betty and I are in the midst of negotiations. I won't mind eating cookies, but not due to a bad situation. If I eat a cookie it will be because I want to enjoy the taste. The whole losing weight business is off the table. She will have to give in on some points too. She won't argue if I go on the cross trainer just to keep fit.

If you think of it, it's hilarious to be discussing matters with your ego. It's a game with Betty. If I put things differently - or even better; if I choose to think differently on matters- Betty stops putting her foot down.

The World According to Josef

Chapter 6 Everything under control Betty?

I've been a structured creature my entire life. Where other teenagers couldn't open their bedroom door because of the pile of rubbish lying behind it, my room was a temple of tidiness. I love a tidy house. It gives me a sense of peace and quiet. When my home is in order, my head is in order. It does have some other advantages, I can tell you. You can walk around the house in the dark without injuring yourself and you never waste time on looking for that one particular item you need before you rush out of the house.

Loving something and holding on to something are two entirely different things. Betty holds on to things. She wants to keep the house clean. It's comforting to her. Holding on to something means having rules. Lots of rules. We put items on specifically chosen places and we put them back in the same place after using it. Things are nicely arranged. It becomes a challenge if Betty allows others in her domain. What to do if a friend walks in and jumps on the couch with shoes on telling you: "Oh my goodness, what a lovely comfortable couch." Betty starts exploding, because she imagines all sorts of accidents on the couch; coffee being spilled and cookies being crunched over it. I often solve this situation by serving coffee at my large dining table, so the visitor gets off the couch to join me. It's a way to avoid an uncomfortable situation. I don't want to be an inhospitable person and I realize it's not a nice feeling for a friend to constantly watch if they're not spilling things on my couch.

I often look at how others deal with this and I notice a difference. It looks like these people are not bothered by the rules Betty seems to hold on to. "Come on in and jump on the couch" is their whole idea. How many rules are there actually in Betty's book? The couch is just one thing, but there are others. Take common courtesy for example. She could write a book about it…

The do's and don'ts on messenger. While we were dating, Betty was very busy with manners, according to her standards. A potential prince charming wrote us some messages and Betty would spent a lot of time reading them with a magnifying glass. The thing she had an issue with was the fact that in the middle of a conversation the man, at some point, ended the chat with five words Betty didn't see coming:

I'm
going
to
bed

Flabbergasted she stared at the little screen. "Excuse me? We are having a conversation and you end it like this?"

I did ask men why they do that. They had no clue as to that being rude. "Well, it's my bedtime so I announce that I'm going to sleep." How else should I say it?" was their response. Of course Betty was more than willing to give them a lesson in how to end a conversation in her perfect way. "Look, you mention that it's almost bedtime soon. Then, you make some small talk, wishing me a good night too. Then you end the conversation. How difficult is that?" she asked. The way men ended a conversation was something from the cave era. Looking back on this, I can't stop laughing. Where did she get the nerve to tell people how to end a conversation? Who was being rude? Betty! I went to get some feedback from women and it was a relief that they felt the same way. That's something an ego will do too, find allies to proof their point.

Where does this urge to control things come from; the need to be the director of a situation, the need to change others so they become more pleasurable to be with? The need to know things up front? I can't think of any other reason than out of a supposed feeling of security.

It is most definitely one of the least beautiful sides of the human being. The need to dominate. That is what it looks like: being in control. If you want to interact with others you may want to find out what the other person wants. Otherwise it will be a lonely walk on the path of life. Funny thing, because I like to interact very much.

I had to find a way to deal with Betty in her unstoppable need to be in control. Betty had transformed 'not wanting things' to an artistic skill. Even if it was just for the reason of not wanting it and there was no clear reason behind it.

Practicing submission became a project. Oh dear, Betty was upset. "You are not going to do what other people tell you? Come on. You've spend years being Miss Goody Two Shoes, placing other people's needs before yours. We decided that we were done with that." Betty had a point there.

Letting go of the need to control things was a bit of a struggle. I'll risk repeating myself in this book, but it all comes down to the way you think about yourself.

One of the first things I tried to let go was wanting to know things up front. Not knowing what will happen is an unpleasant feeling. I think most of us would like a little glass ball to look into the future to see how things will turn out. Sadly, we don't have that little ball and so I started reading a book on how to change your thinking into a more positive way of thinking. I could do that, I figured but of course Betty had an opinion on it. "That would be self-help book number… Help me out, I've lost count through the years." All your precious self-help books are doing on that bookshelf is collecting dust, I could hear in my ear.

I started reading anyway. The Secret. Step one. Think of what you really want. Well, that was easy. I wanted a job where I could earn money to pay my bills, nice co-workers, close to home, with an interesting workload.

Step two. Imagine what you want. I could do that. I saw myself standing in the shower, singing, making lunch to bring to work, leaving for work and having a great day. Step 3. Let it go. Ouch! That was hard. First they make you think of what you want, visualize it until it already appears to be a reality, only to forget about it and just let it go? Betty thought it was a stupid book.

The butting out step was invented for a reason. If you think about what you want too much, you might start having doubts about the result. That way all you were getting was more doubts and the thing you wanted never happened. Betty wanted a guarantee for result. In black and white. Proof that this 'wishing things project' would pay off. Every time we didn't get a job, her mean voice echoed in my ear, pointing out that it was a stupid book. I thought it wise not to mention the fact that the failure of this project was due to the ego.

So, how to let go if the ego wants to hold on and demands proof. The only way you can make it work, if somewhere deep down you have a complete commitment to the thing you want.

But how do you find that one thing you'll have full commitment for? Good question. You may want to look at why you want something. I had been wanting things, because I didn't want something else anymore. That reason for wanting is not effective. That would be like you didn't like spinach and decide to want carrots instead. After a while the carrots will taste just as bad and you would think of yet another vegetable to want. It's like walking around in circles.

The vegetable theory was applicable to many situations. To wanting a relationship, wanting a job and wanting a nice house. If you just wish to get rid of something you don't like, you end up with something else you won't like. That took me a while to figure out.

Another way the ego struggles with control is when something is forbidden. Especially if it's something you are fond of. Habits. One day I needed to have some surgery done. The letter from the hospital stated that I had to be sober before the operation. Oh dear, Betty had seen it too. She started moaning. "Sober?" We always eat straight away once we get out of bed. If we don't we get grumpy. Every day, same routine. Two leaves of bread, chocolate sprinkles, orange juice and coffee, otherwise we aren't ready to start the day. We could make an exception as to what to eat, but we always eat! No matter what.

The day before the operation I wasn't nervous for the surgery. Not at all. I was upset. Upset with the fact that I couldn't eat. Not eating, oh there was a challenge. Betty reminded me nicely as I was eating my breakfast the day before the operation. "This is our last breakfast" I heard in my head. I calculated up to what time I was allowed to eat and I set my alarm to eat my breakfast at that time. It was hilarious. Something as insignificant as having breakfast had become a huge issue.

The day of the operation I sat at the table. Only a few more hours, then I could eat again. I don't know if there are people who work for the Universe, but if there were, they would have laughed their pants of looking at me that day. That day I didn't get to eat until way after dinner time. My operation was scheduled at 12 pm and I didn't reach the operation room until 17pm, due to a lot of emergency operations. I was lying in the hospital bed for hours, in my nighty being sober. Breathing, breathing, breathing. Betty was having a tough time. After the operation, which took ten minutes, I lay in the recovery room. Once

The World According to Betty

I'd opened my eyes, the nurse asked "How are you?" I just said one word: "Hungry!" The nurse smiled. "Would you like a sandwich?" "A sandwich?" "How about six!"

If I look back on this adventure, I have survived almost an entire day without eating. I did it. It's all between the ears… where Betty lives.

Recently I was told not to wash my hair for three days. "Honestly ma'am, please stick to that and don't wash your hair", the nurse told me. "We'll see about that", Betty said. "Filthy hair, I don't think so!" It was Betty who made me stand in the bathroom and only washing the front part of my hair. I had stitches on the back, so that part had to stay dry. Just the thought of having a clean front was comforting to Betty.

There have been numerous occasions where the resistance of my ego came was due to us being told that we were not allowed to do something. Betty wants to decide that herself. Sticking to routines, habits and certainly not changing them because some else says so. Only if there is a very good reason she may consider working with me. Otherwise, she sticks to her way of doing things.

Chapter 7 Revenge

"Revenge is often the confession of having pain".

One of the emotions you may experience from the ego, is wanting revenge. If the ego thinks you have been wronged, it wants pay back. The other must pay for what he or she has done, so the score is even.

Betty has a little black book in her room. In that book are the names of people she would love to settle the score with. People who have belittled us, people who have spoken badly about us behind our backs, people who disabled us to have a promotion at work, people who caused us pain.

I can imagine, for instance, how people come up with a plan to get back at the person who bullied them for a long period of time. I'm not encouraging people to take the law into their own hands, but I can see why they would want to.

Betty usually has a lot to say, but doesn't act on the revenge issue. Somewhere in me there is something that prevents me from acting on feelings of revenge, maybe knowing that it won't solve anything anyway. The person who wronged you won't start liking you and the pain you experienced will not go away.

Eleanor Roosevelt once said that nobody can put you down, unless you give them permission to do so. It's a complicated quote. It takes a feeling of self-worth to let other people's opinions be their opinion and not believe that to be THE truth. If you get hurt by words of others, actually means that somewhere in you there is some self-doubt about what was said. Otherwise you couldn't have cared less.

I often thought, what if… What if one day one of the girls who bullied me would reappear in my life? Say I was to work for the government and I would have a say in the question that would decide if someone could get benefits or not. A position with some power attached. You open a file and see a name and suddenly you're back in school. The mean laughter, the damage to your bike, you can re-call it very clear. What will you do? Put the file under all the others? Make it disappear? I know I wouldn't do it.

I know Betty would run the idea by me. The emotion from many many years ago, will fill my head like a grey cloud. Sure, I'm grownup now, nothing like that will ever happen to me again. I won't let it, but at that time it was life changing for me.

One of the things I did do, in cooperation with Betty is reshaping my life by erasing some people. When we were dating Betty was an excellent eraser of the men who came to court us. After yet again a pointless conversation or the proof that a prince charming had less noble intentions, she had a little finger with no mercy. –Click! - Removed from contacts and that meant from all the places where he had been a contact. The phone, Facebook, mailbox. Hasta la vista, evil prince. See you never again.

From other women I heard that they had red books instead of black books. A red book was a way of parking a man. The ego of the ladies wanted to remove the villain from their phones, computers… but they left a small opportunity open for them to reappear. They wrote down the name, telephone number and some details, like a small archive for unfortunate attempts. For Betty a red book was no option. Delete is delete. No archive.

There was a small disadvantage to the eagerness to erase. It did happen that she would erase a man due to revenge, let's call him Prince X. This prince had made a new profile and she would meet him again online. The prince had no idea that he had been erased and would start a conversation as if nothing had happened. A second opportunity for Betty to get revenge. The 'sorry who are you' method. "Help me out here, I'm not sure who you are". No prince liked being treated that way and as a result ended the conversation offended to the bone.

The need for revenge starts when Betty thinks something isn't fair, or if a hurtful remark is made. The worst of all is that Betty hardly let's time pass to think things through. She reacts instantly and passionate. The emotion is strong and often hard to stop. She needs to respond, she has to. She needs to let a person know that it was not OK or that they were mean. She will open up her little archive of arguments to proof that she has been wronged. No time to think about the other side of the story, no she goes for it.

The big disadvantage is, once the emotion fades the damage becomes visible. Suddenly there is time to reflect, time for shame. "Oops!" I can hear her say. There was another side to the story, there was an explanation. "I'll be damned!" she whispers.

When in need of revenge, one can meet the merciless little witch inside yourself, who seeks allies to think of ways to get even. One time a less reliable man had it coming, when he tried to date Betty and was trying the same with her best friend. The two little egos continued talking to him until it was time to confront him with his dishonest behaviour. Betty and her conspiring friend were playing together. The poor man never saw the attack coming and will remember the lesson that was taught him for a long time.

That was all quite harmless and the little scratches on Betty's soul were easy to heal. It became complicated when some things happened in a work environment.

Betty not only has nasty behaviour. She's also a good protector and a warning system for danger and for other people's egos, playing on the playground called life. A difficult situation arises, when you know something is wrong or there's foul play involved and you don't have proof. For months I searched for a solution in one of my jobs. Betty moaned. She wanted to end a situation in which people were just being very dishonest. I had tried to be open and ask my co-workers about their true feelings and intentions, but they kept denying that there was a problem, unlike the ghosts in my head. It all ended with me quitting my job. A serious decision.

The World According to Betty

On the final day at work, when the office was empty, Betty found proof that she'd been looking for all that time. A complete series of emails. All the things I had been trying to explain to my manager were there. "Told you so, I was RIGHT", Betty shouted. She was thrilled with this evidence.

She almost had her fingers on the keyboard to forward all the information to the manager. "Who do these ladies think they are, talking about me, calling me names and laughing about how they had won?" "Do they think they will get away with this again?" My predecessor had been bullied by them too. They had told me about that. She had left the job with a burn-out.

It was tempting to forward the evidence, but I didn't. I figured that the damage these two ladies had caused would not be undone by me sending this to the manager. I didn't want to stay at an organization where this kind of behaviour was possible, with a manager who displayed nothing but a blurred vision. I decided not to act upon my need to pay them back. I got my things, left the building and closed the door just a tiny bit harder than usual. Betty had left the building… for good.

It wasn't going to be the last time that Betty was ready to throw Molotov cocktails to fight for justice. Unfortunately going to war isn't the solution. If you want to do something about dishonesty in a team, you need to find allies to fight with you. Not everyone is willing to stand up and share their opinion when working in a hostile team.

Letting go of the story and realizing that it's pointless to keep hanging on to it, never crosses Betty's mind. There were times that I went to sleep and I was stuck with an overactive little ego that was very busy having conversations in my head. She talked to the people she accused of things. She told them what she thought of them or demanded apologies. The result of this behaviour was, waking up feeling tired and surrounded by some sort of grey cloud, because of the nightly activity of Betty dearest.

I got fed up with waking up tired because of this emotion. The conversations in my head were not positive and took up a great deal of my energy. I decided to distract my little Betty, by putting on music or positive meditations before I went to sleep. That seemed to do the trick, because I haven't heard her babbling in my head since. Don't worry, she still tries to be heard, during the day.

My need for revenge is nearly gone and I'm on to Betty. I know when and why she feels the need for revenge. We occasionally have a hiccup. The last time she beat me to it, was when someone invited me to be friends on Facebook. It turned out that he had pressed the invite button without even knowing who he invited. After a few days I accepted the invite and within a few minutes there was a message. "I see we've become friends, but I've no idea who you are." At that point I couldn't see the irony... Betty was offended. "You don't know me and yet you press the invite button?" I tried to stay calm. Betty said: "You have slippery fingers I assume?" "Yes, I guess I do" was the response. "Well, you could always de-friend me", Betty said. "I will." That was it. This man was going down.

Betty needed to put her finger on the delete button before he did. In the rush to do so, she pushed the invite button... twice. Steam coming out of my ears... I looked at the screen and suddenly I saw the irony. How many times had Betty done the same thing to men in her dating days…? Maybe the Universe was giving out a life lesson that day. Revenge doesn't pay off… It comes back to you to bite you in your behind.

Chapter 8 You or me?

The English call it the people-pleaser, the system where you're being nice to people just to make sure you're accepted, respected and given the right to exist (in some cases). I kept up with that system for a long time in my life. In this area Betty has been my protector instead of the usual 'pain in the butt'.

Before I knew Betty, I was a nice person, according to my family, friends and neighbours. I tried to keep up with the unwritten rules that society has made for us. Betty was already with me, but I wasn't aware of her. I did experience some strong feelings like a rebel who doesn't like to adjust to society.

Birthdays were somewhat of a torture for me. Having to sit in a room with the same group of people, and the same conversations was not my cup of tea. I felt a constant urge to leave the room, but I couldn't because the room was so packed that reaching the door was practically impossible. The conversations were always about the family, the home, the holidays, the usual. I sat there smiling, but inside me there was a storm coming.

After meeting Betty, she would yell in my ear: "Look at all these people being perfectly happy. We know better." She knew that some of them weren't happy at all, but at birthdays they seemed to be experts in keeping up appearances.

If someone asked: "How are you?" the expected answer would be: "I'm fine." People asked out of habit or politeness. They never meant to really find out how you were doing. Betty wanted to tell them about how we weren't happy at all and make them sit down and listen for at least one hour, so they would hear all the details. But that was not done. It would cause a shock.

So I smiled and answered in the proper manner and tried to keep Betty calm.

In relationships I came across the same subject. You or me. I had put other people's needs before mine for years. I had a great job before I became a mom, but I quit this job to be there for my daughter. I took care of the house and all the social obligations. I started to notice how at the start of each new year I had a moment where I didn't know where I was heading in life. I didn't know if I could call it being unsatisfied or unhappy. One thing I did know, things weren't going the way I would like them to.

Somewhere around thirty eight it happened. I just had 'the question' again. "Is this it? Is this my life?" I had signed up for a training weekend about self-reflection.

It was a training on reversing thoughts. It sounded exciting to me. I enjoyed all the insights and I was on a pink cloud for weeks after I attended. I was on top of the world. Everything was fine. I was at peace, until I fell of the cloud when the effect of the training wore out.

After that weekend I kept visiting a coach to get my life in order. I made a deal with myself that I would lose weight. I took up yoga classes. I started leaving my comfort zone by connecting with people on the internet. I started to change. I finally started doing things I liked.

After a while the people around me reacted to my change. They didn't like the fact that I was becoming a different person. The old me was fading. I started to do things for me. I started educating myself in subjects I liked, but they didn't get what I was doing. Sometimes I struggled with that. I wasn't able to show the complete version of me to the world. The world seemed to have a problem with that. They wanted me to stay the way I was before.

My new appearance and the space I wanted for myself, finally lead to a divorce. Betty had just been 'born' and she was going wild.

"I like a wife who is home by the time I get home from work" I can still hear my former husband say these words as we were standing in the kitchen. Betty was yelling in my ear: "How about that… we've gone through all this trouble to change and we finally look nice and love ourselves and he wants us to pull out our wand and undo the magic?" "I don't think so!' The 'you or me-question' was put on the table. I couldn't do it. Going back to my old version. I choose me with all the consequences I couldn't foresee. I don't know if I would have made the same decision, if I had known what was coming, but at that moment I just decided.

After the divorce the 'you or me question' occurred several times. Finding a new partner wasn't easy. I took up the old habit of giving to be liked again. Not a smart thing to do once you have a Betty living in your head. She would comment merciless if yet another attempt went bad.

"I told you so, they are all the same. They're only coming to get the pleasures of life and afterwards the wave goodbye. It's never about you, always about them." Betty wanted to put her little hands around the necks of men. She was fed up with them.

It took me some time to realize that giving with an expectation to receive wasn't the smart thing to do. I ended up in a difficult relationship with a very complicated man. I had made a very impulsive decision to move in with him, due to the fact that I had to leave the home I had lived in during my marriage. The 'you or me question' had been on the table regarding who would stay in the house after the divorce.

I wanted a peaceful way to settle the divorce so I gave up a lot of things. Once it became clear that my husband wasn't going to leave the house, I panicked and ran into the arms of a man who said he offered to jump in an adventure with me. Sure it wasn't a very wise move, but given the circumstances I didn't see any other option. If it was me today, I would have fought, I would have claimed things, I would have done things differently.

The man I came to live with had a specific way of thinking about life. He started to tell me that people should love themselves unconditionally. I soon found out what he meant by that and how he was testing me. He put me in situations where I had to make choices. Me or him, me or my former husband and me or my child. It felt like boot camp in a psychological way. Betty was screaming and hurting. This wasn't what we wanted in a relationship. This wasn't loving and caring for a woman. After six months I had had enough. I wanted out. The only problem was, that I knew if I wanted to leave he would make me move out that same day. How would I get my things out of the house? Those words kept going round and round in my head. I felt scared to say anything about wanting to leave the relationship.

I found out I was being tested by him when I took my daughter on a trip. I had been given some money by my former husband to pay for outings. My new partner didn't agree with that. He didn't want me to take it. Once I arrived at the resort he called and asked if I had taken the money. I told him the truth. He was angry. The arguments kept going all evening on the phone, until the moment I told him I had enough and was done with him. He texted me after that. "Congratulations…you finally passed the test." "Now you know what it's like to love yourself unconditionally." I stared at the phone. I was outraged. All I had been to him was a project.

I remember sitting at the table in his house on a Monday morning, thinking about my life. This was not the way I wanted it. I was so unhappy. I might as well pack up and leave. I would be alone, but less unhappy than I was at that point. I packed my things and drove away, not knowing where I would end up that day. Betty was scared. She was terrified.

The funny thing about making a decision is that it provides room for new opportunities. I found a home for myself that same day. I started a life for myself. Betty was very upset with the man we had lived with. After a while I started thinking, if I hadn't met him, I wouldn't have ended up where I did. What he tried to teach me was to stop being a conditional giver. He tried to make me stand up for myself. The theory was all right, but the way he tried to teach me wasn't. The you or me question had been an adventure.

You might think I had had my lesson. I did go and live with another man after that. The idea of someone taking care of me was important. I had felt abandoned in my life several times, so psychologists will certainly blame the moving in with these two men on that history. This relationship wasn't as rough as the one before. I got out must faster and moved back into my old house eventually. Betty was relieved. No more moving in for us. We would have our own castle from now on.

The relationships I had aren't something I'm proud of. Betty had a wall of shame in her room, where these situations are written down. Just in case I might get silly ideas again. She will remind me of past mistakes by pointing at the wall.

Looking back I can see I needed to experience these situations to stop needing someone to take care of me. I found my own safe haven with me. We are quite happy living on our own. That's what the 'you or me question' period has given us. We think about us before we make a move.

Chapter 9 Betty and Sherlock

It was inevitable that Betty would find a new relationship one day. After all her adventures on dating sites and all the men she had given a piece of her mind... Sherlock came into our lives. Needless to say, it's wasn't a slow motion scene where we would run into each other's arms whispering the words "Where were you all my life?" No. Nothing like that... It was a bumping in to each other, which might have been a short one, if it were up to Betty.

How Betty met Sherlock...

Just when Betty was done with the entire male department of the human race, Sherlock came along. "It's OK to just have a chat", he said. Nowadays we seem to order everything online, so why not a potential partner. Betty was just about to reach for the delete button with a heavy sigh, as I realized... maybe this guy has a point. A chat can't hurt us. Not all men are the vicious hunters we've known some of 'm to be. I ignored Betty and responded to his remark. That's wasn't a bad move, we are still talking, for many years now.

One might think 'all's well that ends well", but then you would have forgotten the presence of Betty dearest. A Sherlock in our lives is nice, but Betty was sounding the alarm in her majestic tower in my head. "Let's not be hasty! Let's see if this Sherlock is to be trusted! Let him proof his loyalty and pure intentions to us!"

Sherlock had no idea that he hadn't just met me, but another 'woman' as well. I don't know if he would have been so happy, if he'd known about Betty upfront.

The first months Betty was busy with her investigation. There were challenges like the differences between me and Sherlock. Plus the fact that Sherlock had become aware of the little diva in the tower. He had some trouble dealing with her. It took me some time to explain Betty to him; why she was there and what her function was. I had to make sure he didn't take me for a person who would be better off in an environment for people with multiple personality disorder.

Sherlock had one big advantage, he had the ability to stay calm under most of the circumstances. No counter attacks, no discussions. Betty's attempts to start a war were useless. The 'enemy' did nothing. A tantrum would die a slow death, because of the lack of attention for it.

I keep referring to him as Sherlock, but my newfound love had no idea of the little character inside him and that he was to be named Sherlock. That was after some time, once the bumps in the road of the relationship became clear; feelings that weren't shared and assumptions on what the other might think. Just when Betty was about to call it a day things started to change.

The World According to Betty

The selection of the character wasn't that hard for my boyfriend. His fondness of researching, collecting information triggered by a word or a conversation in combination with his somewhat clumsy way of communicating, made the choice for Sherlock Holmes obvious: clever, yet incomprehensible at times.

The relationship is holding up, due to the fact that of each of us have our own world. Past experiences have taught that putting together two families is a big challenge and I'd been there, done that and am not going there again. It's nicer to be able to miss a partner during the week and once reunited to be able to share stories together. Besides, I had learned to enjoy being on my own during my adventures, so having my own space was a non-negotiable item. That's how we ended up having a weekend relationship.

Sometimes Betty and Sherlock communicate directly with each other. We are in contact every day through WhatsApp and a conversation like this is quite common:

Hey Sherlock

Yes Betty

Do you feel neglected?

Yes. What are WE going to do about it?

Conversations like these are hilarious and effective; it makes saying what you normally wouldn't say so much easier. Giving feedback about less attractive habits is not as hard that way.

Betty and Sherlock are quite different. The extrovert Betty is sure to keep life exciting and the introvert Sherlock looks at the little lady with astonishment.

"What do you think?" I ask. "Is this a nice shirt?" The situation: shopping for outfits for the cruise we were about to enjoy together. Sherlock is standing in between clothing racks with his smart phone in his hands. I can see that he pushes a button on the screen. He loves to play a game online. Something with villages and attacks.

"Tsss, men will always be boys" Betty says while she walks towards the next row of clothing in her distinguished way. A few seconds later the answer to the question follows: "Oh sure, that looks fine" Sherlock says. Betty sighs. "What kind of advice is that, a useless one, that's for sure?"

Shortly before, I had been to the men's department with Sherlock to find suitable clothes for him. He had our undivided attention, although we were tempted to peek at the ladies department. But we didn't. We were focused and how did he repay our attention?

"Well as long as you're planning your little war, I might as well go to the fitting room", Betty said in her evil voice. Sherlock followed her to the fitting room and waited outside on the 'husband bench' that stores put there for the men who are dragged to the store to pay or to give advice which will not be appreciated anyway. "That's what you get from eating too many cookies" I hear inside my head. "I try to get the shirt on, but the reality hits me quicker than I would have liked it to. I blame myself for my weakness for cookies and step out of the fitting room.

The World According to Betty

"It doesn't suit me, does it?" I ask. "Well, that's not too bad", he tries carefully. He knows Betty by now. "It's just that it doesn't fit nicely on the back". "Men!" Betty sighs and marches right back to the fitting room, pulling the curtains a little harder than necessary. Sherlock knows he's doomed whether or not he says something. It's not easy living with Betty.

As Sherlock made his appearance at the royal Betty court, she measured him to see if he would meet up to her high expectations. I can assure you, he failed miserably. While having tea with her friend Miss Piggy (the ego of my best friend) Sherlock was being analysed. "Well I don't know..." Betty sighed. "What's wrong?" "Well, you know, I don't know, how shall I put this, he's ... different." "Didn't we agree that the perfect man doesn't exist ages ago, Betty?" "I know, I know. I shouldn't make such a fuss. He's nice and sweet, doesn't have sweaty feet and he's quiet. Actually there's nothing wrong with him..."

Miss Piggy squeezes her eyes in an investigative manner. "I feel a but coming, Betty." "Yes, it's just... well he's so different and he communicates different." "Well duh, it's a MAN!" "Nooo, it's not the undeveloped things we all know men have. Or haven't to be exact." Betty takes a look at her well organized list and picks one subject. "Take the other day for example. He's standing in the kitchen, being so sweet, making home baked bread. Suddenly he walks to the dining table and sits down at his laptop to review the recipe with his hands covered in dough! I mean, honestly, is it that much trouble to wash your hands?"

"Betty, aren't you just searching for things that are wrong with Sherlock, just because you can?" Miss Piggy nods as if she knows she's right. "I mean, isn't it just very scary to finally meet a decent guy?"

That was indeed the case. It was a whole new concept finding a man who accepted us as we are, made an effort to understand us and refused to go to war with Betty. That must have been the most annoying thing about Sherlock: Betty couldn't start a war, because Sherlock didn't send his troops (like he does in his game online) instead he just kept quiet and did nothing.

Betty was having trouble with the fact that Sherlock seemed to accept her presence unconditionally. It made her grumpy and she started to think: "He can accept us and we can't do it! Darn, that's irritating!" It took some walking up and down her room, leaving marks on the carpet, before Betty could accept the little things that were wrong with Sherlock. The thing that helped most was a sense of humour.

Sherlock is in the kitchen. "Honey, I'm making meatballs, just the way you like them." As I walk to him to see what he has made I see the scale. "I guess one could apply science on cooking?" I teasingly ask him. "Yes, if you weigh the meat and divide it through the amount of balls, you will get equally sized balls." Betty rolls her eyes. "You're joking?" No, Sherlock was being dead serious. He likes it. He's the scientist, the man with a preference for being precise. Betty finds that awfully exhausting. She has no patience what so ever. "You just throw the meat in a bowl, add the content of the little bag from the prefixed package with one egg, mix it and you're done." Such a comment makes Sherlock feel like the floor has been broken down from under his feet. Betty puts her arms in front of her chest and sounds determined: "Why bother with weighing, that's too much trouble!"

I have come to see the funny part of it by now: Sherlock and his perfect meatballs, nicely weighed and tasting delicious. Betty is not fond of differences, because there is a risk of things not going the way she wants them to go. It took a lot of effort to get her to let things be. Weighed balls, different views on what a tidy kitchen looks like (although Sherlock tries his best to leave the kitchen spotless after baking bread). Betty has an uncontrollable urge to go in with a cleaning cloth after he leaves and clean the scale (which he always puts back dirty and that's just disgusting complains Betty).

Her Majesty the Queen should offer Sherlock the title 'Sir', don't you think? He has put up with Betty's behaviour for several years. Betty has gotten used to Sherlock and is willing to make an effort to accept his ways and giggle about the meatballs.

The presence of Betty and Sherlock in our relationship has proven to be effective. It provides us with an open way of communicating. Arguments are part of our lives and that's fine. We both know that they are caused by the little characters inside us. We have a lot of fun with them and that gives us the chance to lighten things up a bit.

The ego in a relationship, it's an interesting subject. One could easily write a book about it, don't you think? Who knows... to be continued?

Chapter 10 "Honey, is that your mother in the freezer next to Ben & Jerry?"

"What is it in another person, that irritates you about you?"

Betty looks at the quote and moans. "Sure, of course, it's always my fault. So if I get irritated by other people's behaviour, I'm to blame?" I don't think so!"

Looking at your own emotions in reaction to what other people say or do is difficult. When I looked at the quote, I had a manager I couldn't stand. A reoccurring pattern as I would found out later on. The manager was a small man with a big car. "Well, someone is compensating for something", Betty thought viciously. "His ego must be so big, he needs a big trunk to transport it."

The thing that bothered me the most was his bossy way of behaving towards the staff. I couldn't understand that he probably had a reason for his behaviour and I didn't care at that point. Maybe his length made him act like that, because he had been bullied at school and now he had made it this far up the ladder he wasn't going to let people put him down…He wanted to be acknowledged, I guess.

The trainer of one of the workshops I attended had handed me the quote. She saw me struggling with it. "What does this boss of yours do that irritates you so much?" she asked. "He's making sure everyone sees how important he is. He want us to recognize him for the great man he is, well he's not. He's a little man!"

"Alright, that may be true", she said, but if you look at you in all honesty, isn't it true that you dislike him because you want to be recognized too?" I thought this trainer was talking rubbish. "No way, that isn't me."

Later on, after discovering Betty, I understood what the trainer was saying. I was acting just like my manager. I acted up, looking for approval, wanting to be seen and heard as well. It hit me, hard. Me, the loving person I thought I was, acted exactly like this manager. How could I be that ugly and look like him?

It would take other difficult bosses to really make me understand this lesson. It was true. The behaviour of others, that I disliked so much, was inside me. Due to Betty.

With this new knowledge I started paying attention to the people I disliked. What were they doing, what were they saying, what was there attitude? In other workshops I specifically sat next to people I thought weren't my cup of tea. The funny effect of that was that after the workshop I usually became friends with them. I told them upfront I had trouble with them and my honesty was being appreciated, most of the time.

This new information about myself was lovely, but there were still people in Betty's little black book I couldn't be nice to. Betty stuck to her opinion. "Those people aren't on my forgiveness list and that's final!"

Sometimes you get free lessons from life when you are struggling with a situation. In my case this meant I got a lesson in forgiveness. I can assure you, Betty is a tough student.

I had been given the task to write down the name of the person I needed to forgive, put it in a bowl of water and into the freezer. I like practical experiments, so one day I did all that. The thought behind this task was to put the nasty thoughts about the person on hold and you would get some space to think about things.

Weeks after the experiment I hear: "Honey, is that your mother in the freezer next Ben & Jerry." I couldn't stop laughing. I had completely forgotten my mother in the freezer. This wasn't a great way to forgive.

The next project was to write down the name of the person you wanted to forgive. The letter would start with "Dear... I forgive you for..." and then you could go wild. All the things you blamed that person for, all the nasty thoughts found their way through my pen to the paper. I wrote and wrote, everyone in the black book was mentioned. "This is fun!" Betty shouted. She was having a field day.

Once the letter of forgiveness was finished, you could burn

it, so the negative thoughts would vanish. Alright, I went looking for the grill in the garden and it appeared to be at a friend's house. I was determined to see this through, so I took a pan, put the letter in it and lit it. Within minutes the garden was filled with smoke. My neighbours weren't amused by my need to train my ego...

But how to forgive, if all the practical experiments seem to be failing? Back to the drawing board.

In the meantime I did notice that I wasn't becoming happier by holding on to the nasty thoughts about people. It seemed that I kept finding myself in the same situations over and over again. There would always be a boss or a fellow human being to irritate me and I guess that I have myself to thank for some of the blame.

Not forgiving, is like putting bars on your own life, I read somewhere. I had to chew on that one. The situations that kept reappearing made me sad. I really needed to take a look at my own behaviour.

Forgiving is not saying that it's alright what the other person did, but choosing to let the story go.

It seemed that Betty had the biggest problem with that: the fact that the other person got away without punishment if I were to forgive them. That would be a silent approval of what they did. "They did do mean things to us. Should we just forget about it? What about justice?" Betty was screaming.

There is one person with whom I haven't been in touch for several years. I remember the day we had our last conversation. I left the room with Betty screaming and shouting in my head. "What are they thinking? We're not going to bow and do as they please." I sat down later on and thought of a way to deal with this situation. I decided to write a letter offering a period of contemplation. I thought I had written an openhearted letter and made sure that Betty stayed out of the conversation on paper. The reaction to my offer was that the other person never wanted to see me again. I guess the letter was opened with an ego reading it too.

If you want to forgive you need to be willing to look at the other side of the story. If you can do that, you find compassion. I found out that the person I've been out of touch with has a right to see things in her own way. The only problem was that the expectations towards me were high. Betty saw the expectations as claiming and she won't stand for that.

The next thing I did was to try and let the story go. I tried to do so without anger. I have written several cards at special days like birthdays and Christmas. Every time I said the same thing. Whatever is between us, I still love you. I get cards back from the other person with the same message.

You might think, if we are communicating through cards, why not try and fix the situation. Well, guess who's talking? Right, Betty. She still has an issue with what happened. This wasn't the first time we had this problem. The old experiences are being brought up every time I try to think about taking a next step.

Do you want to be right, or happy? A quote that I was confronted with many times. This battle with my ego has been going on for some time now. She isn't ready to give up yet. The hurt when being told what to do resides too deep in me. If I look at the other person's feelings, than I see the same hurt. It all comes down to recognition for the feelings you experience.

This situation is in progress. I'm still working on it with Betty. I keep sending the cards and my love and I hope I will get strong enough to solve it.

Forgiving is a process of letting go of the hurt, the anger, the accusations.

Another way in which forgiving plays a role in our lives is the forgiveness we grant ourselves. There are times when I look back and think about all the things I've been through. I haven't always made the best decisions. A part of Betty is guilt; feeling guilty about the things I have done.

I came across a book in which the author explained that everyone makes choices with the knowledge they possess at that point. I was so glad to find that story. That made sense. If I had known better, I would have acted differently. That is when you find compassion towards yourself.

Betty is an expert at pointing out our flaws. We did have a period of adventure when we wanted a relationship so badly. We were naive at some point. We did get distracted and struggled with distinguishing to what was important from what wasn't.

Looking back, makes me realize that if I hadn't made mistakes, I wouldn't have learned things the things I've learned. The person I've become is born out of all the hurt and pain and disappointments I've experienced. I'm grateful for the fact that I had the chance to get to where I am today.

Forgiving myself did remove the bars from my live. It increased my self-esteem. I started to value the things I've done and the lessons I've learned.

Chapter 11 Betty is moving out

I have boxes in the room. I put the little bits and bops in it. "Let me think, what else does she need?" In the room inside my head I can hear her soaking. She is upset. She is angry. She is furious. She knows what is coming and she's fighting me.

I continue packing and the moaning goes on and on. She fights for her existence, her opinion, and her thinking patterns. Betty is giving me a speech: "I have always protected you, haven't I? I made sure that WE were safe or at least drove people away if they threatened us! I have been sharp as a knife to people who cheated on us and look at you…you are packing my things? Thanks for nothing!"

I ignore her shouting. It's time an it's been for a long time, but I now knew it had to be done. The tantrums, the monologues, the negative thinking, they are moving out. I feel they no longer serve me. Betty is fading. She feels it and she's resisting. She wants to stay, wants to hold on to what felt safe, but it's time, she made me sad too often.

How many times did I figure out that it was Betty who

got me into trouble? A nasty manager who put us down, according to Betty, it showed me a perfect mirror of what I had to do. I had to change my way of thinking and start believing that I was a great employee. I got the opportunity to see my talents. If I received feedback, I learned to thank the person for it instead of feeling useless. Making mistakes is human, not learning from them is worse. Betty, however, was ready to throw stones at the manager. "What was this Barbie-look-a-like thinking, with her blond hair and her ego? Criticising us, no way!"

Every time Betty was about to explode I saw that the alleged enemy was striking back even harder. Letting Betty do the talking was absolutely pointless. From that moment on, as I decided to ignore Betty, things changed. The manager didn't seem to look for opportunities to catch me on making a mistake. She even had a compliment in store for me!

The battle with Betty was rough. I knew I had to ignore her, but sometimes she was stronger. It's like being in rehab; letting the ego be what it is. It takes time. There are so many old thinking patterns and believes stored in the ego. Betty has a complete archive with footage of past experiences. "Remember… when…" followed by the complete story with all the pain and suffering we had gone through.

Betty writes her own fairy tale. The story 'Once upon never…' A dream of prince charming on his horse always ended abruptly due to Betty and her negative thinking pattern. She is sabotaging every opportunity of being happy, because she doesn't believe in happy endings. She refuses to see the story of 'Yes we can'. The reason Betty does this, is because of the lack of self-confidence or self-esteem. The lack of believing in us; in our dreams and opportunities.

Often Betty saw the edge of the cliff. "Oh dear!" she would moan. "Will we ever get out of this situation?" Every time there was a little miracle that saved us, usually caused by my habit to keep repeating that it would be alright. Betty would curl up on her couch with a blanket and a cup of tea, shivering with fear and doubts, waiting to see if the miracle would arrive. She is my biggest protector and my worst enemy at the same time. Believing in the story of 'Yes we can' feels like playing bluff inside your head. You never have proof upfront to show you that the miracle will actually take place.

I fetch more boxes, this time for all the diaries from Betty. The bookshelves in her room have taken up a lot of space. With her elegant pen she would write down all our emotions and adventures. She kept score of who had to be paid back. That way, if a similar situation occurred with someone, she would have all the former details to make sure she had a weapon to defend us against getting hurt again. So sweet of her, but not very practical. I threw all the little diaries in the box. They can go. Time to clean up.

I go to her, take her fragile hand in mine and say "Betty, it's time." She looks at me with her big eyes and sobs. "I have decided you're moving out of my head." "I acknowledge you as my ego, but not as a leading person in my head; you can have your own apartment elsewhere." I hug her and say: "Thank you for all your trouble while of taking care of us." You meant well, I know, it's just that I can take it from here. Goodbye dear Betty." She picks up her suitcase and walks out of my head, on her way to stay somewhere where I can see her, but won't be hearing her all the time. I will keep in touch, but it will never be the same again.

Sometimes Betty comes to visit. She will have a cup of tea and watches what I'm writing about her on my website. She sighs. She is content. "A book about me!" Egos do like attention and acknowledgement. If she starts making a fuss about things, I keep it short and simple. I only have to say: "Oh dear, look at the time, shouldn't you get home?" She knows that she needs to be quiet then and leaves.

Afterword

"How does it feel to write a book, madam author? Put that in writing for me, will you?" my coach asks me. The first word that came to mind was Bangerang, the expression of total bliss from Peter Pan in the movie Hook. It feels like a dream coming true due to me believing in it.

Writing a book with Betty as a co-author was quite the challenge, you will understand. She made life extremely difficult. Try and concentrate if someone keeps whispering: "Are you seriously considering writing that?" "Suppose people are going to dislike you for your honesty?" Betty was like a mosquito in the bedroom while you're trying to sleep. Totally irritating, driving you to get your fly killer and smack at every bit of air around you, until it's quiet again.

While I was writing chapters it seemed like there was something mysterious in the air. Every time I picked a subject to write about, situations around that subject started to happen. You can imagine what happened when I started the Revenge chapter! That's not my favourite emotion to be handling. I did collect enough knowledge on Betty to know that there always will be situations to face where she'll be nagging me.

Writing this book convinced me even more of the fact that my thoughts about myself matter. I have become more aware of my thinking patterns and know that my ego isn't the director of my life anymore.

My editor asked me: "What does this Betty of yours think of the book? Wouldn't it be great if she granted us an interview?" I felt a giggle coming up and my imagination was triggered. I can hear her now…

"Well, I would like to use this totally unexpected opportunity to thank the following people…" (Grabs her black book with the title 'List of settling score').

"Thank you, Henri dear! (The ego character of the banana incident). I can tell you that these days my bananas are kept outside the fridge, because it was MY idea to do so and maybe you might have had a point there (coughs) but that's beside the point at this moment."

We would like to thank the man who made us into his personal project and wanted to see us pass the 'love yourself unconditionally exam'. Thanks to him we now know what we don't want in a relationship and we have experienced that even if we think all hope is lost, there are always new doors opening if you just are brave enough to let things go.

Thanks to the man who made us see that we are much more loveable when living on our own and that combining families hardly ever works out.

The World According to Betty

Thanks to all the managers we've had that made us sigh and hold our breath until we finally realized that we are good enough as we are. It just took some believing in ourselves.

Thank you, all the princes on white horses on the dating site. I hope by now you all have found a princess with a flexible calendar, who loves spending time alone on Christmas Eve and Thanksgiving.

Thank you, dearest Piggy, my best friend also known as Mieke, for all the times we laughed, cried and yelled together. But most of all for all the fun I had with you.

Sherlock, darling... thank you for your outstanding way of ignoring me. As the Dalai Lama says: "Silence is so much more powerful than words." You have proved to be a worthy opponent during all my tantrums, impatience and moments of insecurity that took me by surprise. You have shown yourself in your vulnerable way and offered to invent yourself to court me...

(By the way, you haven't forgotten our anniversary again, right? And please no boring bouquet of flowers this year!)

I think we will have yet another falling out about the Holidays I so dread, but lucky you, Ernestine is well trained and will reward my behaviour with a cold shower to cool me of.

Hm, maybe I have something to say too, Betty dear...

"Well if you insist..."

"I do!"

"Well, darn… okay, the stage is yours!"

(Rolls her eyes)

I would like to thank everyone who has motivated me to keep going and make my dream come true. It's sort of a weird subject to write about and not everyone will get the idea or will be thrilled about it. However, there were people who were willing to believe in me and Betty from the first moment.

Peter Kaagman (a.k.a. Sherlock), my rock and IT specialist. Thank you for all the research on how to write a book. Thanks for all your patience to work with me and Betty.

Brian Canavan, coach an author at Optiva Coaching, who continued to kick my charming behind to keep going on the book.

John White, my biggest fan and the first Englishman/ Aussie who read my book. Without John and his support I wouldn't have been able to make it as beautiful as it now.

Deniece Wildschut, my editor, who started laughing from the moment she started editing and helped me with fine tuning the content.

Jolanda Kranenburg, my creative friend who helped me with the design of the cover and Jeanet (Jolanda's ego) who had become best friends with Betty.

And at last (certainly not the place she would have picked…) Betty. Thank you for all the irritation, the frustration, the endless whining and crying… Without you, this book would not have been written. Thank you darling!

Just a sec

"Hold your horses!" "Don't close the book yet!" "If I may have your undivided attention?" "Thank you so much, dear reader." "I do love attention, but that's something you might have discovered by now."

"Alright Betty, go ahead, but keep it short, will you!"

"I've got some great news!" "There's a second book coming!" "Unfortunately I'll have to share the stage, but hey some things can't be changed (although I'll try my best to succeed in changing them). "The next book is about ME and Sherlock. "What it's called?"

"Ladies and gentlemen, with great pride I announce that the next book about me (and Sherlock) will be called:

"Betty and Sherlock" (Egos in a relationship)

Here's a sneak peek:

"What's that you're watching on You Tube?" I ask, as the voice of an American speaking man finds his way into my living room. He looks up from his laptop. "Oh, that's a tutorial about knives" and he turns his attention to the laptop again. I should have known, his fascination with knives is triggered once again. I soon found out about his love for knives, after meeting him. He has a miniature in his pocket with lots of gadgets and that's beside the collection he has at home. I guess it's an instinct of nature, passed on from generation to generation, starting in the early cave ages. Betty looks at him and wants to sigh. She has her opinion on him being tutorial-happy, and with him she means Sherlock. Out of the blue he pushes a button to watch a video and a stream of information starts to fill up the room, just as our creative flow started to write a blog about some happy subject. At a following incident Betty gets up, walks to a cupboard, and pulls a headset out of drawer, closing it just a bit harder than necessary. With a lot of theatrics she starts to wiggle the tiny end of the cord into the laptop, not doing a great job, due to the irritation she had built up in the moments before. Meanwhile two eyes are watching Betty's behaviour from across the table. "Am I bothering you?" he asks in a calm voice, very wisely ignoring Betty at that point. I need to stop her, I need to shut her up before she starts talking viscously. With some effort I manage to say: "Oh not at all" and suddenly the end of the cord finds its way into the laptop, enabling me to shut the world out (and Sherlock for that matter) and shutting Betty up in the process.

This is just one of the many examples of the adventures Betty has with Sherlock. In the book "Betty and Sherlock" the author takes you on a trip inside her head and the head of Sherlock to show you what happens if you put two egos together, with full awareness of their existence. Knowing about your ego doesn't give you a guarantee for a long and happy life. It takes some work to get to the happily ever after part. Just as in "The world according to Betty" the book is filled with juicy quotes from Betty and the reactions from her opposite in crime Sherlock. Where Betty loses her nerves, Sherlock is the introvert one, with the occasional implosion.

"Betty and Sherlock" is just as "The world according to Betty" an Inspiration Book where there reader is invited to look around, laugh and maybe recognize things and then decide whether or not to do something with the content.

"Well, I would like to thank you for your attention and we'll meet again in the next book..."

"Thank you Betty."

www.ingramcontent.com/pod-product-compliance
Lightning Source LLC
Chambersburg PA
CBHW050542280326
41933CB00011B/1692